MEGA BOOKS

RESCUERS

CHRISTIANE GUNZI
AND CHEZ PICTHALL

Gareth Stevens
PUBLISHING

BE A SUPER SPOTTER

Study these pictures and look out for them as you read this book. Can you answer the super spotter questions?

Which rescuer has these stripes?

Which rescuer runs on these tracks?

Which rescuer is blowing snow?

Which rescuer has this propeller?

Please visit our website, www.garethstevens.com. For a free color catalog of all our high-quality books, call toll free 1-800-542-2595 or fax 1-877-542-2596.

Published in 2025 by
Gareth Stevens Publishing
2544 Clinton St.
Buffalo, NY 14224

Written and edited by: Christiane Gunzi and Chez Picthall
Designer: Paul Calver
Editorial assistant: Katy Rayner
Vehicle consultant: Gary Boyd-Hope

Thank you to the following companies and individuals for the use of their images: AugustaWestland; American Emergency Vehicles (*www.aev.com*); All Wales Ambulance Services; Automobile Lamborghini SpA; Chrysler Group; Don Winslow Photography (*www.donwinslow.net*); Flying Tankers Inc.; Galloway Mountain Rescue Team (*www.gallowaymrt.org.uk*); Gerard Donnelly; Getty Images; Ives Group; J. Godwin – Emergency Vehicles Online (*www.fire-appliances.com*); Jige International; John Dennis Coachbuilders Ltd; Kris Walker, Oceanid; Leavesley International; Maarten Visser/CC BY-SA 2.0; Mader International Pty Ltd (*www.mader.com.au*); Maritime and Coastguard Agency; Metalcraft Marine Inc. and City of Seward, Alaska); Michael Martinelli; Mike Evans; National Science Foundation – Emily Stone, Kristen Hutchison, Patrick Rowe; Oshkosh Truck Corporation; RNLI/Nicholas Leach and Graeme Sweeney; Scania Image Desk; Service de police de la Ville de Repentigny; Shutterstock.com (Marcel van den Bos); Steve Bailey, Gibbs Technologies; Thrandur Arnthorsson from *www.4x4offroads.com*; Tim Webber, Edale Mountain Rescue; U.S. Coast Guard; Volvo Car Corporation; Yuba City Police Department

Cataloging-in-Publication Data

Names: Gunzi, Christiane. | Picthall, Chez.
Title: Rescuers / by Christiane Gunzi and Chez Picthall.
Description: Buffalo, NY : Gareth Stevens Publishing, 2025. | Series: Mega books
Identifiers: ISBN 9781482468052 (pbk.) | ISBN 9781482468069 (library bound) | ISBN 9781482468076 (ebook)
Subjects: LCSH: Emergency vehicles--Juvenile literature. | Rescue work--Juvenile literature.
Classification: LCC TL235.8 G86 2025 | DDC 629.225--dc23

Printed in the United States of America

CPSIA compliance information: Batch #CSGS25: For further information contact Gareth Stevens at 1-800-542-2595.

CONTENTS

FIRE ENGINES

A fire engine is a big emergency vehicle that puts out fires. It has hoses on board and an extra engine for pumping water. Some fire engines also carry ladders, axes and fire extinguishers. The team of firefighters spray water on the fire.

Big and bright

Fire engines are big and red so that they are easy to see. This fire engine has blue lights on top that flash on and off.

Water power

Most fire engines have room for up to six firefighters on board. One firefighter drives the engine, one firefighter pumps the water, and the rest use the hoses.

Can you point to?

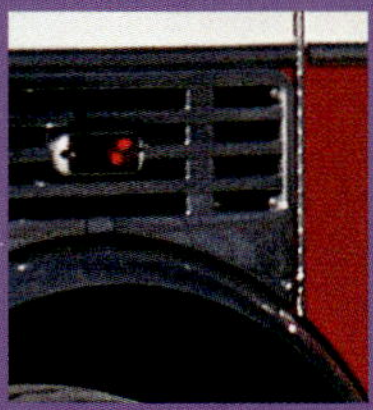

a number

some lights

a badge

Fighting fires

This type of fire engine can put out fires with water, powder, and foam. It is used in cities and also for forest fires, and it can easily drive through narrow gaps.

Mega load

The engine below carries 500 gallons (1,892 l) of water. It has enough room on board for six people.

How many firefighters can you see?

FIRE TRUCKS

A fire truck is a rescue vehicle that has ladders, ropes, special tools, a medical kit, and rescue equipment on board. A fire truck that also contains a tank of water is called a "quint."

Truck with telescopic ladder up

Mega tank

This big fire truck is a quint. It has enough room inside for 10 firefighters and can easily carry 3,000 gallons (11,356 l) of water in its tanks.

Safe buildings

This Supervac truck is used in New York. If a building or some scaffolding collapses it races to the rescue. There is a lot of special equipment on board.

Off-roader

This tough fire truck can drive on rough ground, through mud, and up steep slopes to rescue people. The truck's bodywork is high up off the ground.

Can you find a bell anywhere?

Dangerous materials

The truck above is used when there is an accident with hazardous (dangerous) materials. This truck is full of all sorts of rescue equipment, but it does not carry ladders, water, or a hose.

AIRPORT RESCUERS

Rescue vehicles at airports need to be tough and fast. They may have to drive over slippery ground or through water. They often have six wheels and are very powerful. They carry water and foam on board, and can put out any kind of aircraft fire.

Red racer

This truck goes from 0 to 50 miles (80 km) an hour in 25 seconds! It can drive over any surface at an airport.

Can you point to?

a badge

a number

a foot step

Airport truck spraying water

Where can you see a fire?

Mega tank

Airport rescuers carry up to 11,900 gallons (45,000 l) of water in their tanks. Some have 450 horsepower engines.

Super truck

This truck has big windows to help the driver see clearly. It is fast, can go through water, and is even able to climb over low walls. It is called a "Striker."

Oshkosh® Striker® putting out a fire

AMBULANCES

These important vehicles rescue people and rush them to the hospital. Ambulances have loud sirens and flashing lights to tell other traffic to get out of the way. Inside there is room for patients, paramedics or doctors, and emergency equipment.

Six wheels

This special ambulance is used by the UK's Royal Air Force. It has six wheels and can drive up steep hills and over rough ground.

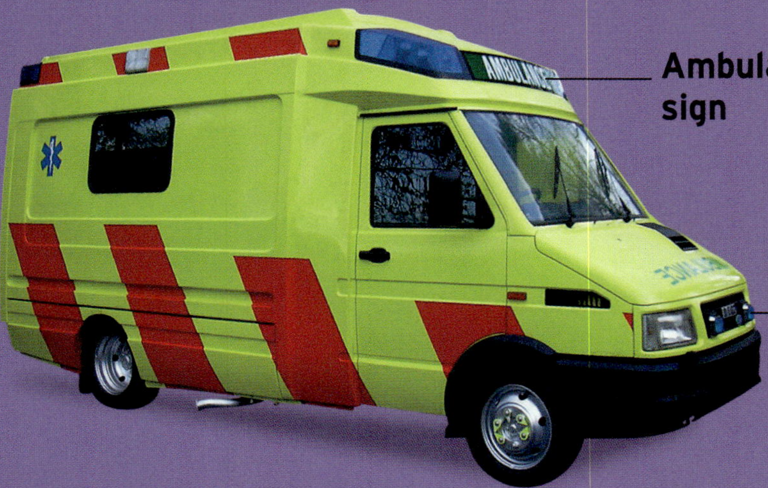

Which ambulance has six wheels?

Colorful rescuer

Ambulances are usually yellow and red, or white and red so that people can see them easily. They often have chevrons or other patterns along the sides to make them stand out more.

Speedy bike

This fast bike is used by the Ambulance Service in the UK. It it able to come to the rescue quickly in cities, where an ambulance might get stuck in a traffic jam.

Can you point to?

an aerial

a badge

some squares

Fire rescuer

This fire rescue ambulance has lots of rescue equipment on board. It can carry two patients and two firefighter paramedics.

Rapid response

"Sprinter" ambulances like this one are used all across Australia.

POLICE CARS

Police cars do dangerous work so they have to be powerful, tough, fast, and safe to drive. A police car has flashing lights and loud sirens to warn other traffic to move out of the way.

Electric power

This electric police car is used in Canada to patrol in the city and keep it safe. It can travel up to 185 miles (300 km) on one charge!

Checkered car

In the UK, police cars can drive more than 62,000 miles (100,000 km) every year patrolling roads and highways. These cars have patterns on them so that other drivers can see them clearly.

Smart police car

Little cars like this one are used for lots of jobs, including visiting schools to teach children about police work.

Danger van

This special vehicle is used for dangerous jobs, such as hunting for criminals who have weapons. The police who use it are very well trained.

What job does the little police car do?

Lamborghini

This sports car was used by the Italian police. It could go from 0 to 60 miles (96 km) an hour in about four seconds and it had a top speed of 192 miles (309 km) an hour!

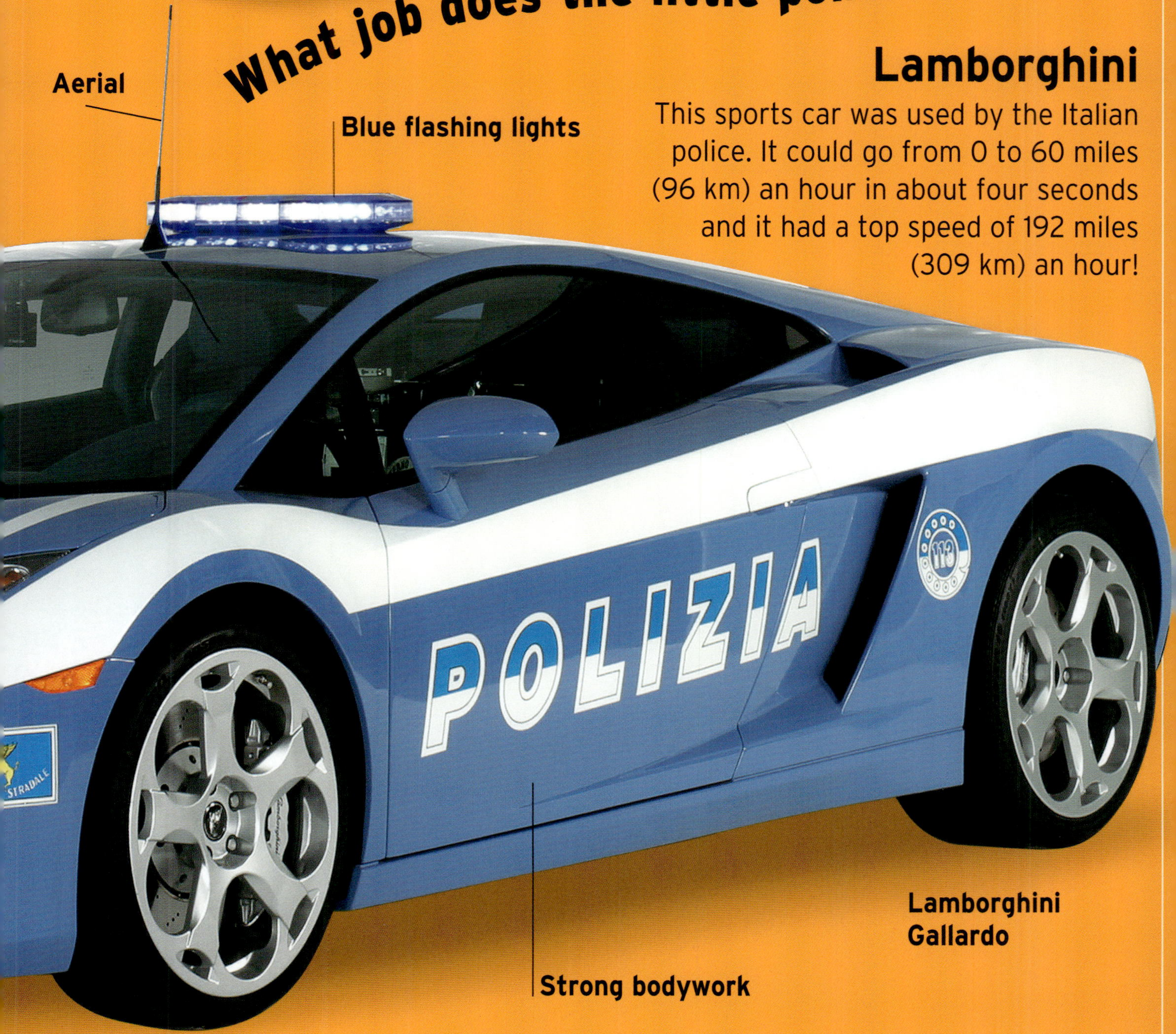

Lamborghini Gallardo

RECOVERY TRUCKS

When a car, truck, or bus breaks down or has a road accident, a recovery truck goes to the rescue. These big, strong vehicles can pick up broken-down vehicles and tow or carry them home.

Can you point to?

a number

a logo

a hubcap

Rescuing a car at the beach

Car carrier

The Volvo car carrier above recovers cars and trucks by carrying them away on its back.

Wreckers

This truck is called a wrecker. It has large stabilizers at the sides, called outriggers. These keep it steady when it lifts heavy vehicles. These controls can be operated from the driver's seat or the passenger seat.

Can you find a picture of an alligator?

SNOW CLEARERS

Fast, powerful snowplows, snowblowers, and snow brooms keep the roads safe for traffic in winter. These rescue trucks have to work very quickly. They also clear snow off runways at airports.

Snow machine

This snowcat runs on tracks which help it to drive over the snow. Machines like this one are often used to keep ski runs clear.

Snow broom

This snow broom has two engines. The engine at the back moves the machine forwards, and the one at the front spins the broom to brush away the snow.

Snowblowers

These snow machines have very powerful engines. Some snow blowers can clear 8,270 tons (7,500 mt) of snow an hour, shooting it out at the sides as they go along.

Which of these snow vehicles drives on tracks?

Snowplow

This vehicle's curved plow is 23 feet (7 m) wide. It pushes snow out of the way as it drives. It also pulls along a big broom that sweeps away any snow that is left behind by the large plow.

MOUNTAIN RESCUERS

If someone has an accident on a mountain it is difficult for an ordinary ambulance to reach them. Off-road vehicles can drive up steep hills and rocky tracks to rescue people.

Lots of equipment

4X4s like this Land Rover carry all sorts of equipment, including radios, stretchers, powerful lights, satellite phones, and a medical kit.

Land Rover Ambulance

Can you point to?

a circle

squares

a grille

Nissan Patrol

This powerful car is used in snow. It has searchlights, a radio, telephone, air tank, cables, a winch, a towline, stretchers, and avalanche sticks!

Jeep

The Jeep above can rescue people in deserts as well as up mountains. The roof slides open, the windshield folds, and the doors come off!

Can you find a searchlight?

Mountain ambulance

This is a very special kind of ambulance. It has lots of computer equipment inside to help find people when they are lost.

AMAZING RESCUERS

A few rescue vehicles can drive almost anywhere to reach people. They go up mountains or through rivers. Others can drive on snow and ice. Every year, thousands of people are saved by these amazing vehicles.

Going anywhere

The vehicle below drives on rubber tracks. It can go anywhere, even through water. It is so big that it can seat up to 17 people inside!

Snowmobile

This speedy snowmobile has tracks at the back and skis at the front so it can drive over snow and ice. It is often used for rescuing skiers.

Tracks on the ice

This vehicle can drive on ice and is used by scientists in the Antarctic. There is a hatch in the roof so that passengers can escape if it falls through the ice.

Can you point to?

a rectangle

a circle

a driver

Land and sea rescuer

Lifeguards use these special quad bikes to help people in emergencies on beaches if they are swept out to sea. Its wheels fold up inside, just by flicking a switch!

Can you find the snowmobile?

RESCUE HELICOPTERS

Helicopters rescue at sea, on the seashore, and up mountains. They are quick and can get to places that other rescuers cannot reach. Helicopters are also used for putting out fires.

Super searcher

Helicopters like this one have powerful searchlights to help them find the people they need to rescue. They can carry up to 5.5 tons (5 mt) of emergency equipment on board.

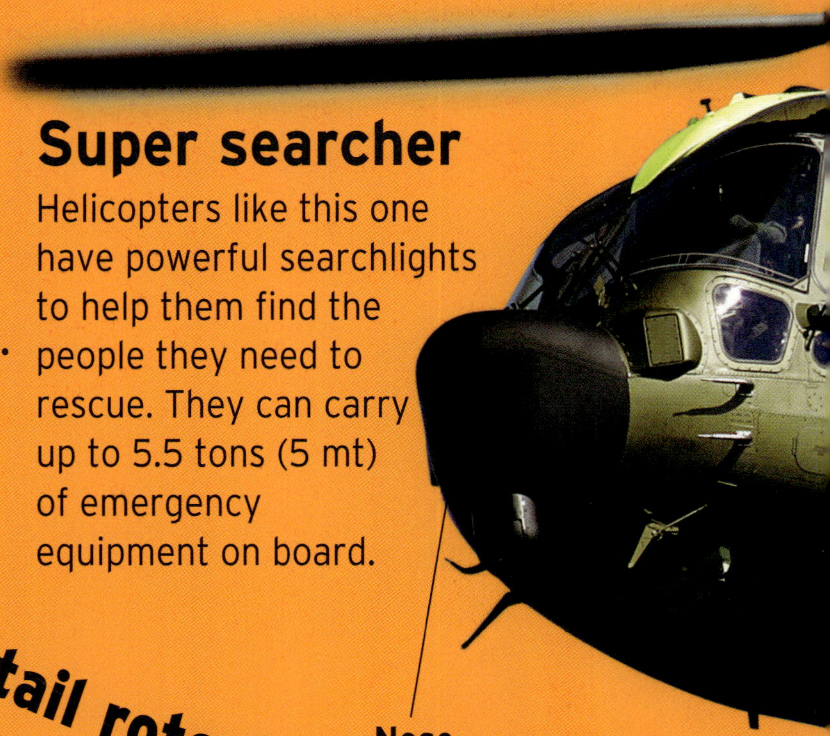

Can you point to the tail rotor?

Rescuing a person on a stretcher

Up and away

The helicopter on the left has a hoist on the side so that it can lift people up and away from danger.

Mixed up

This rescue aircraft is a mixture of an airplane and a helicopter. It can fly in bad weather, and it can also hover. It can fly fast and rescue people far away.

Can you point to?

a cross

a number

some letters

In-flight treatment

In the helicopter below, the cabin is separate from the cockpit. Doctors can travel in the cabin with the patient, and treat them while the helicopter is flying them to the hospital.

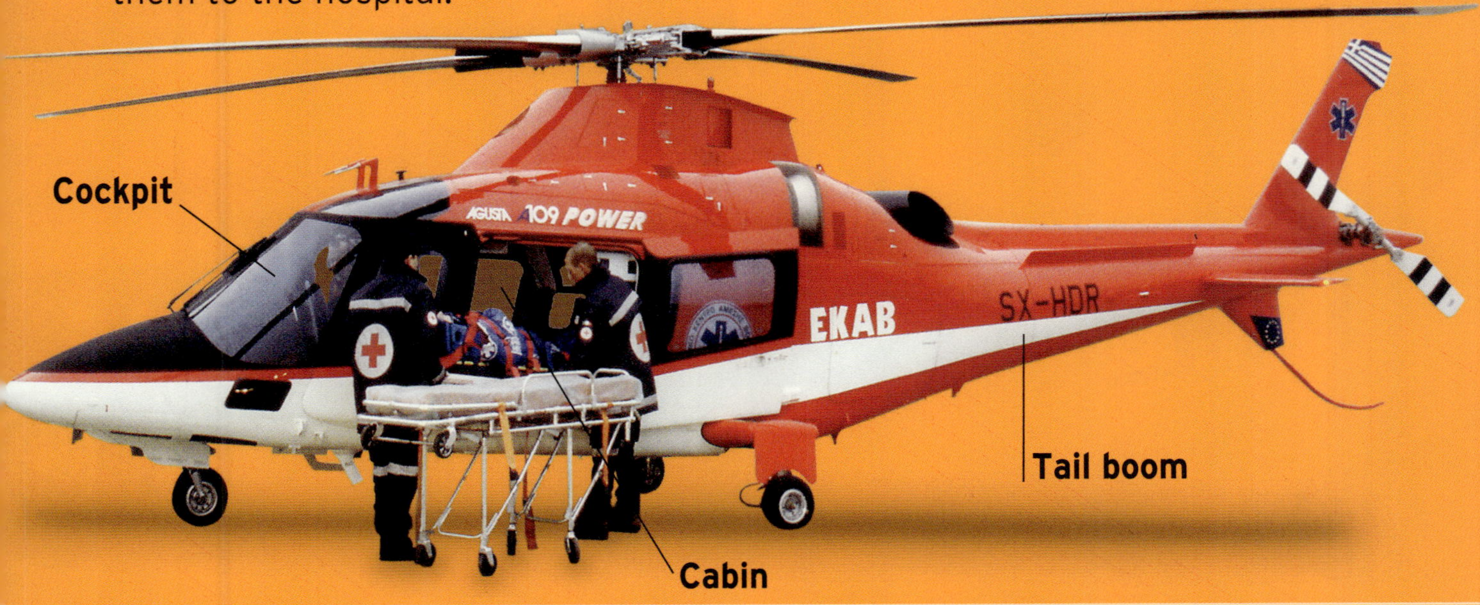

AIR TANKERS

In forests and other wild places that fire engines cannot reach, airplanes called air tankers carry water and a special liquid for putting out fires. They fly high above the trees, spraying the fire.

Water bomber putting out a forest fire

Super Scooper

The flying boat above can scoop up 1,620 gallons (6,140 l) of water from the sea or a lake and drop it onto a fire, then refill to do it again without returning to base.

Can you point to?

letters

some stripes

numbers

Air tractor

This firefighter can fly at 220 miles (356 km) an hour. It is useful for putting out fires in small areas. Airplanes like this one are also used for spraying farm crops, so they are also called air tractors.

Flying firefighter

The air tanker below is used for putting out fires in forests and in the countryside. It flies at up to 280 miles (450 km) an hour and carries 1,200 gallons (4,542 l) of liquid for fighting fires.

Can you point to the pilot?

FIREBOATS

A fireboat is like a fire engine on water. It has pumps that suck in water and then shoot it out to fight fires on ships and sailing boats. Fireboats carry lots of special fire and rescue equipment on board.

River rescuer

Small fireboats like this one can travel up narrow rivers to put out fires on other boats. This Firestorm boat goes at 42 miles (68 km) an hour, and pumps hundreds of gallons of water every minute.

Can you see a funnel?

Firestorm boat

This tough Firestorm fireboat has emergency lights, a fog horn, and a siren. There is also a room in the cabin for treating people who are being rescued.

Firestorm fireboat putting out a fire

Can you point to?

a ring

a number

some steps

Mega fireboat

This big fireboat is used by the Los Angeles Fire Department. It is 115 feet (35 m) long and can pump over 37,000 gallons (140,000 l) of water. It has eight firefighters on board.

SEA RESCUERS

Lifeboats rescue people on boats out at sea. They often have to go out in a storm, so the work is very dangerous for the crew. Lifeboats are fast, tough, and powerful.

Water stretcher

The yellow rescue boat above is a blow-up stretcher that floats on water. It used in the sea, and on lakes, rivers, ice, and snow.

A boat that hovers

A hovercraft glides easily over water, sand, and mud, so it is useful for searching along the seashore. At the back are two fans that work like airplane propellers.

Rigid inflatable boat

These powerful boats are also known as RIBs. They are strong and stable and can go fast, even in rough seas. This one has two big engines.

What color is the hovercraft?

Motor lifeboat

The amazing motorboat above is used for rescuing people at sea in very bad weather. It is almost unsinkable and can turn itself upright in less than 30 seconds!

Sea searcher

Small, fast boats like this are used by coast guard services to patrol the sea and rescue people. They are designed to work even in tall waves.

ICEBREAKERS

An icebreaker is a huge, powerful ship that moves through icy waters. It clears ice out of the way for other ships, and it helps other boats on rescue missions. Icebreakers are a special shape and can move backward as easily as forward.

Clearing a path

The Russian icebreaker called *Krasin* is famous. It helped the U.S. Coast Guard to clear a pathway through the ice in Antarctica. It broke up the ice so that other ships could follow behind.

Mega icebreaker

This U.S. icebreaker is called the *Polar Star*. There is room for 35 scientists and two helicopters on board. It also has a shop and a library. The *Polar Star* can push through ice 20 feet (6 m) thick!

Can you point to?

a letter

a lifeboat

a flag

Super ship

An icebreaker is very strong. Propellers at the front and back push the ship forward. The ship drives onto the ice and is so heavy that the ice breaks underneath it.

GLOSSARY

Aerial – a metal rod or wire by which radio signals are sent and received.

Chevron – V-shaped markings used on emergency vehicles to make them more visible. They are often light-reflective, so they can be seen easily in the dark.

Cockpit – the place at the front of an airplane or helicopter where the pilot sits to fly the aircraft.

Emergency – a serious event or situation where people's lives or property are at risk. Fast response to these events can often save lives.

Locker – a compartment on the side of an emergency vehicle where important equipment can be kept securely.

Off-road vehicle – a vehicle that is made to be driven on rough or rocky surfaces. It will usually have large tires with deep treads.

Paramedic – a person trained to give medical care to people in an emergency. Paramedics do not work in hospitals but travel in emergency vehicles to help people who have been hurt or suddenly become ill.

Radar – a system that uses radio waves to detect ships, aircraft, and other objects. It also shows their distance, direction, and speed, which helps with search and rescue missions.

Satellite phone – a telephone that uses space satellites to allow communication in remote places.

Searchlight – a powerful light that is used to find missing things and people in the dark.

Telescopic ladder – a ladder that can be attached to, or carried on, a truck, and can be extended to reach and rescue people in tall buildings.

Winch – a very strong rope or chain that winds around a rotating drum and is used to lift or haul objects or people.

INDEX